EAST

Program Builder
Number 20

**Plays—Skits—Songs
Recitations—Exercises**

Compiled by
Diane K. Cunningham

Permission to make photocopies of program builders
is granted to the purchaser when three books have
been purchased. The photocopies cannot be sold,
loaned, or given away.

Lillenas Publishing Co.
KANSAS CITY, MO 64141

Welcome, One and All

I am as happy as can be,
Standing here so tall,
For I have an Easter wish:
Welcome, one and all!

—*Kathleen Leighton*

I Think I'm Big Enough

They wouldn't let me say a rhyme
Like bigger children do;
But I think I am big enough
To say "Hello" to you—
(smile)
And "Happy Easter," too!

—*Dorothy Conant Stroud*

Easter Joy

Easter morning, Easter joy—
God's gift to every girl and boy.

—*Kathleen Leighton*

Stand Tall

I want to stand up here,
Stand very tall on Easter Day;
"Jesus is my Savior,"
That's all I have to say—
(starts to leave)
Six more words I have to say:
"I love Him more each day."

—*Helen Kitchell Evans*

Glorious Easter Day

Christ arose on Easter Day;
An angel rolled the stone away;
Oh, glorious Easter Day!
Oh, wonderful Day!

—*Helen Kitchell Evans*

Dressed Up

I'm all dressed up, as you can see,
To speak my piece for you;
And God dressed up these flowers here
For Easter morning, too.

—*Phyllis C. Michael*

Beauty

Every flower at Easter
Seems to say to me,
"Jesus gave this beauty
For all of us to see."

—*Helen Kitchell Evans*

I Want to Shine for Jesus

(A child carrying a tiny candle comes to the platform with the entire Beginner Department. When all are on the platform, the one carrying the candle steps to the front and recites.)

Easter is a shining day,
As bright as candle glow.
It makes me want to shine for Jesus
Everywhere I go!

(The group can then sing "This Little Light of Mine.")

—*Margaret N. Freeman*

Light Hearts

The sun is high
Up in the sky,
    Like a smile on Easter Day.
It's a happy sight
And our hearts are light,
    As we walk in Jesus' way.

—*Rega Kramer McCarthy*

Not There

The tomb is empty,
    Jesus is not there;
He has risen on Easter Day,
    His love with us to share.

—*Helen Kitchell Evans*

Easter Light

Easter light is shining clear;
Easter blessings now draw near;
Easter songs are on the air;
Easter joy is everywhere.

—*Margaret E. Chenot*

What You Need

You do not need a lot of clothes
    To get God's Easter favor;
You need to know that Christ arose,
    And take Him as your Savior.

—*Vida Munden Nixon*

Truly, Sincerely

Truly and sincerely,
    From a heart of love,
I wish you Easter blessings
    Straight from heaven above.

—*Vida Munden Nixon*

Happy Thoughts at Easter

(An exercise for eight children)

Unison:
    Happy thoughts at Easter
        Fill our hearts with love,
    Thinking of the Savior,
        Risen Lord above.

First Child:
    Thoughts of resurrection,

Second Child:
    Thoughts of life and light,

Third Child:
    Thoughts of heaven's sunshine,

Fourth Child:
    Where there comes no night,

Fifth Child:
    Thoughts of hope and gladness,

Sixth Child:
    Thoughts of lasting peace,

Seventh Child:
    Thoughts of joy eternal

Eighth Child:
    That shall never cease.

—*Vida Munden Nixon*

All Things Are New

All things are new,
    And hopes are bright;
The sun breaks through
    With morning light.

All things are new
    This Easter morn,
For it is true
    I've been reborn.

    —*Vida Munden Nixon*

My Walk with Jesus

Every morning just outside
    I can hear the robins sing.
They are bursting now with song,
    For they seem to know it's spring.

And the flowers are popping out
    On the mountains—valleys too;
It's a lovely time for walking
    And that I often do.

When I see new life is coming
    To nature everywhere,
Then my thoughts all turn to Easter,
    And right then I breathe a prayer.

Then I think how Jesus gave His life,
    And I long to touch His hand,
And to hear Him speak so softly,
    And then I understand—

Understand about salvation,
    What Jesus means to me;
And I say to Jesus as I walk,
    "I will live for Thee."

    —*Helen Kitchell Evans*

The Meaning of Easter

(An exercise for six girls. Each girl should carry a cardboard cross with one letter of the word "Easter" pasted on the upright section. The cross should be covered with white paper. The letters should be made of purple art paper.)

E—Every time we think of spring
    Our praise to God we all should bring.

A—A prayer of thanks we now begin,
    To aid Him who came to save from sin.

S—So glad we are to know for sure
    That Jesus died to make us pure!

T—The best part of the story goes
    Like this—our Lord arose!

E—Each little blossom seems to say,
    "Look up and sing. It's Easter Day!"

R—Rejoice, all children everywhere!
    His love for us we all may share.

Unison:

"For God so loved the world, that he gave his only begotten Son, that whosoever believeth in him should not perish, but have everlasting life."

    —*Bula K. Pope*

Son of God

They took You in the garden
  And You answered not a word
When Peter tried to save You
  You said, "Put down your sword."

They mocked You in the trial
  And shouted in the din.
Pilate gave his judgment,
  "I find no fault in Him."

They killed You on Golgotha
  And hung You on a tree.
A believing Roman soldier said,
  "The Son of God is He."

—*Eleanor W. Cunningham*

It's a Joy to Welcome You

We are glad to welcome you
  At this Easter time so bright,
In the name of Him who rose
  And banished Calvary's night.

May all of Easter's joylight,
  Its blessings, sunshine, too,
Bless as you worship with us,
  And bless coming days for you.

—*Margaret N. Freeman*

Welcome

We are so glad to see you!
  I'm sure you'd never guess
How much your being with us
  Adds to our happiness.

Of course you know that Easter
  Christ rose from the tomb
And that He lives forever
  To banish sin and gloom.

If you will make Him welcome,
  Right in your heart He'll stay,
And you will learn why Christians
  Are joyful every day.

—*Pearl Neilson*

Come Along

(An exercise for seven children. Each carries a large letter. When placed in proper order the letters spell "He Arose.")

H Happy, happy Easter Day,
E Everyone rejoicing!

A Anthems ringing far and near,
R Righteousness are voicing.
O Oh, the joy of this glad day!
S Sing aloud hosannas.
E Everyone gives forth His praise;

Unison:
  Come along and join us.

—*Melba Pennock*

Thomas

Jesus appeared to others
  Behind the doors of the room,
His friends could not deny it,
  He rose up from the tomb.

But doubting disciple Thomas
  The truth could not receive
Until he saw the nailprints
  (points to palm of hand)
  Then Thomas, too, believed!

—*Eleanor W. Cunningham*

The Soldier

(Boy may be dressed as a Roman soldier with helmet, sword, and shield.)

I was the one on guard that night
  When the stones began to shake;
I was the one that was filled with
    fright,
  When the earth began to quake.

They said to say I was asleep,
  That disciples stole Him away,
But I was there at the empty tomb,
  Christ *arose* that glorious day.

—*Eleanor W. Cunningham*

Easter Time Reminds Us

(The children enter singing "Christ the Lord Is Risen Today." Adult choir and congregation may sing with them as they enter. They go to front of church for their presentation.)

Choir 1: Easter time reminds us
 That our Jesus lives;

Choir 2: Easter time reminds us
 It's Jesus who forgives.

Unison: Wonderful, wonderful Easter
 When Jesus did appear;
 From the tomb He arose
 To save each person here.

Choir 1: Easter time is beautiful
 With springtime in the air;

Choir 2: Easter time brings lovely
 flowers,
 Scattered everywhere.

Unison: Wonderful, wonderful Easter
 When Jesus did appear;
 From the tomb He arose
 To save each person here.

Choir 1: The church bells ring so
 sweetly
 On a beautiful Easter Day;

Choir 2: They call us all together
 To worship and to pray.

Unison: Wonderful, wonderful Easter
 When Jesus did appear;
 From the tomb He arose
 To save each person here.

Solo 1: Be glad! *(low tone)*

Solo 2: Be glad! *(medium tone)*

Solo 3: Be glad! *(high tone)*

Unison: Sing of His great worth!

Choir 1: Let all the earth rejoice!
 Let no one this day be sad.

Choir 2: Let all the earth rejoice!
 Let all the earth be glad!

Unison: Wonderful, wonderful Easter
 When Jesus did appear;
 From the tomb He arose
 To save each person here.

Solo 4: God bless us all this Easter
 And on every day;

Unison: May He shower His bless
 ings
 Upon us as we pray.

    —*Helen Kitchell Evans*

Every Day, Too

If I had stood there by the Cross
 The day that Jesus died,
Would I have left Him hanging there?
 My Jesus, crucified?

It was for me; He took my place
 So I could always live
With Him in heaven forevermore.
 What a beautiful gift to give!

I'm glad that Jesus rose again,
 I love Him, 'deed I do.
And I know that He loves you and me
 On Easter and every day, too.

    —*Phyllis C. Michael*

Glorious Was That Morning!

All the night
Was filled with sorrow,
There was weeping,
There was fear;
Now the dawn
Was softly breaking
When the angel
Did appear.
Now comes heavenly hope
To mortals
For the Resurrection's
Here.
Oh, how glorious
Was that morning
When the Savior
Did appear.

    —*Helen Kitchell Evans*

6

Easter

Child 1: Each of us loves Easter,
      The day that Christ arose;
      Each of us loves Easter,
         Now why do you suppose?

Child 2: All the day brings joy
         To family and friends;
      Love for one another
         That never, never ends.

Child 3: Sometimes we gather for a
         meal,
      We share each other's days;
      We go to church together
      To sing to God our praise.

Child 4: The children enjoy the out-
         doors,
      We romp in the springtime
         air;
      Older folk sit and talk—
      Grandma is glad we're
         there.

Child 5: Everyone seems so happy
      At this time of the year;
      There's more joy, more
         laughter
      When Easter time is here.

All: Rejoice! Rejoice! It's Easter!
      The resurrected Christ
         now lives!
      He loves each one of us—
      Christ loves, and He for-
         gives!

(The first child carries a scroll long enough to reach across in front of all of them. On this last line the fifth child takes the end of the scroll and unrolls it across the front of them. Or, each child can carry a letter that spells Easter, and all lift their letters at the end of the recitation.)

                —*Helen Kitchell Evans*

Spring Awakening

I heard the purple crocus sing,
   "Wake up, you sleepyhead!
Come on, get up, you tulips, now,
   Get up! Get out of bed!"

I watched the tulips slowly rise
   And stretch their leafy arms;
I knew that soon, yes, very soon
   The world would share their
      charms.

In Easter dress they, too, would call,
   "Wake up! wake up! It's spring!"
I knew, for faith woke in my heart,
   I, too, heard the crocus sing.

                —*Phyllis C. Michael*

Resurrection

Child 1: Darkened moon,

Child 2: Night of gloom,

Child 3: Evil's doom,

Child 4: Christ entombed.

Child 5: Gone the night,

Child 6: Morning light,

Child 7: Glorious sight,

All (raise hands high):
      Resurrection might!

                —*Eleanor W. Cunningham*

Were You There?

A Choral Reading

by Phyllis C. Michael

Scene 1

GIRL 1 *(to Peter):* Aren't you one of Jesus' disciples?

PETER: No! I'm not.

(Voice in background imitates rooster crowing.)

GIRL 2: I *know* that I saw you with that man Jesus.

PETER: You are mistaken. I do not even know Him.

GROUP: Surely you are one of them. You are a Galilean.

BOY 1: Yes, you were, too, with Him.

GROUP: Don't you remember that He said He could destroy the Temple and rebuild it in three days? You *were* with Him.

PETER: I do not know the man! *(Voice in background imitates rooster crowing. Peter hangs head and cries as he goes to the other side of the platform.)* Oh, dear Jesus, what have I done? What have I done?

(Two disciples meet PETER.)

DISCIPLE 1: We all promised to stand by Jesus no matter what they did to Him.

DISCIPLE 2: We didn't even go near the place where they took Him.

PETER: I remember that Jesus said I would deny Him three times before the rooster crowed twice. I just can't believe I would do such a terrible thing. Now they will probably torture Him.

GROUP *(in background):* Crucify Him! CRUCIFY HIM!

8

Scene 2

BOY 1: Let's ask that they release Barabbas from prison.

PILATE: What should we do with this man, Jesus?

GROUP *(in background)*: Crucify Him! CRUCIFY HIM!

PILATE: What has He done so terrible that you want to do away with Him?

GROUP: He says He is the Son of God.

PILATE: I think He is innocent. If we crucify Him, it is your fault, not mine. I wash my hands of the whole thing.

GROUP: Crucify Him! CRUCIFY HIM! Release Barabbas!

Scene 3

GIRL 1: Why would they want to harm Him? He never hurt anyone.

BOY: Look! They are putting a crown of thorns on His head!

GIRL 2: Oh look! They are hitting Him. Hard, too! Why must they do that?

GROUP: God has promised to be with us all. Jesus said He must die for our sins.

BOY: Why must He do that?

GROUP: Because He loves us so. We must remember that always.

Finding Easter

A Puppet Play

by Wanda E. Brunstetter

Puppets: Mr. Chicken, Miss Goose, Kitty, Buster Bunny

MR. CHICKEN *(entering):* Cock-a-doodle-do! I feel like a young rooster today. It must be spring fever. I've been working so hard all day that I think I deserve a little nap. *(Lays head down.)* That feels better.

MISS GOOSE *(enters, wearing a bonnet with a flower on it):* Mr. Chicken, wake up. *(Nudges him with her beak.)* Wake up, wake up.

MR. CHICKEN: Cock-a-doodle-do! Oh, it's you, Miss Goose. What do you mean by waking me up from a nice nap?

MISS GOOSE: I'm sorry, but I need your help.

MR. CHICKEN: My help? What do you need?

MISS GOOSE: I'm looking for Easter, and I haven't been able to find it anywhere.

MR. CHICKEN: Easter? You're looking for Easter?

MISS GOOSE: That's right. I even bought a new bonnet.

MR. CHICKEN: Why did you do that?

MISS GOOSE: I thought that if I bought an Easter bonnet, I would surely find Easter.

MR. CHICKEN: I think Easter has something to do with eggs. Let's go find Henrietta Hen and see if she knows where Easter is.

MISS GOOSE: That's a very good idea. She has lots of eggs, too.

(Both puppets exit.)

KITTY *(enters, carrying and licking a lollipop):* Yum, yum . . . this lollipop is so good. I could eat candy every day. I have some gumdrops in the hay loft. Maybe I'll eat those next.

(MR. CHICKEN *and* MISS GOOSE *enter.)*

MR. CHICKEN: Kitty, what have you got?

KITTY (*moving away quickly*): No you don't, Mr. Chicken. You're not getting any licks off my lollipop!

MR. CHICKEN: You have nothing to worry about, Kitty. Lollipops aren't one of my favorite things to eat. Now, if it was some nice crunchy corn seed, or some scraps of lettuce . . .

MISS GOOSE: Kitty, Mr. Chicken and I have been looking for Easter, and we can't find it anywhere. Can you help us?

KITTY: Where have you looked so far?

MISS GOOSE: I wore my Easter bonnet all morning, but I couldn't see Easter anywhere.

MR. CHICKEN: We looked at all of Henrietta Hen's new eggs too, and Easter wasn't there either.

KITTY: I know—candy! That's it, Easter time means candy . . . lots and lots of it.

MISS GOOSE: Do you really think so?

MR. CHICKEN: Let's all go out and get a big bunch of candy, and then see if we find Easter.

KITTY: That's the best idea I've heard all day!

(*All puppets exit.*)

BUSTER BUNNY (*enters and looks around*): I wonder where everybody is. The barnyard hasn't been this empty since one of Henrietta's old eggs got stepped on. Boy did that smell bad! May it rest in peace.

(KITTY *and* MISS GOOSE *enter.*)

KITTY: Buster Bunny! Are we glad to see you!

BUSTER BUNNY: You are? How come?

MISS GOOSE: We have been looking for Easter.

KITTY: You're a bunny, so you must know where Easter is.

BUSTER BUNNY: You can't just go out and *find* Easter.

MISS GOOSE: You can't?

BUSTER BUNNY: No. Easter is a special day. It's not a place. It's a time that is set aside to celebrate once a year.

KITTY: Now I remember! We celebrate Easter by hunting for Easter eggs and eating lots of candy.

MISS GOOSE: And by wearing our best Easter bonnet.

BUSTER BUNNY: That is how some people celebrate Easter, and it is lots of fun to do all of those things. But there is a better, more special reason to celebrate Easter.

KITTY: Better?

MISS GOOSE: More special?

BUSTER BUNNY: That's right. Christians have been celebrating Easter many, many years. It's the day that Jesus rose from the dead. The Bible tells us that after He was killed, He stayed dead for only three days, then He came back to life.

KITTY: Is this why we should celebrate Easter?

BUSTER BUNNY: That's right. On Easter morning people go to Sunday School and church to sing about Jesus and praise Him, because He is up in heaven now making a home for all who give their lives to Him.

MISS GOOSE: That does sound like a much better reason to celebrate Easter than wearing my silly old bonnet.

KITTY: Or getting sick on too much candy. I'm sure glad we talked to you, Buster Bunny.

MISS GOOSE: That's right. We might have spent a long time looking for Easter.

KITTY: Let's go find Mr. Chicken and tell him the good news too.

BUSTER BUNNY: Happy Easter everyone!

(All exit.)

Lives That Touched Jesus

An Easter Presentation for Juniors and Teens

by Cora M. Owen

Scene: *A garden with an empty tomb and a cross in the background. Use fresh plants and flowers for the garden. Background could be made of a drawing, a mural, or actual props. Characters should be dressed in appropriate costumes. They may remain on stage after speaking, or exit if preferred.*

READER: There were many people who met Jesus, and many who knew Him intimately as a friend and companion. Lives that touched His were never to be the same again. I would like to introduce you to some of those people who were with Him during the time of His death and resurrection. They played a part in our Savior's final days on earth. Meet them now.

(Enter JOHN. Stands near the Cross.)

JOHN

I was once a fisherman
　　Who left my nets and all
Just to follow after Him
　　When I heard His call.

I was seated at His side
　　When we had come to sup.
I could hear the words He spoke
　　When He had served the cup.

I'm the one who stayed with Him,
　　I stood beside the Cross;
Took His mother for my own,
　　To help her bear her loss.

I am His disciple, John,
　　Whom Jesus loved the best.
I was at the empty tomb
　　Ahead of all the rest.

13

(Enter JUDAS. *Stands at far side of the scene.)*

JUDAS

I am Judas who betrayed
A man I called my friend
With a traitor's kiss of shame.
No good did I intend.

Through the garden path I walked,
With soldiers rough, I came.
Sent this Jesus to be tried,
Then I was filled with shame.

Took the silver I was paid,
And threw it to the ground;
Then I wept with bitter tears,
But no forgiveness found.

(Enter PETER. *Stands at the tomb.)*

PETER

I am Simon Peter who
Three times my Lord denied;
Then I wept because I knew
I failed when He was tried.

I am Peter, I who ran
Into the tomb that dawn
Saw the linen clothing there
And knew the Lord was gone.

I am Peter, I who said,
"I love You, Lord, You know."
Then He told me, "Feed My lambs"
My love for Him to show.

(Enter PILATE. *Stands near the Cross.)*

PILATE

I am Pilate who could find
No fault in Him at all.
Yet I gave Him to the mob,
Demanded with loud call.

I am Pilate who was weak;
I did not take a stand.
Then I tried to wash away
His blood from off my hand.

I am Pilate filled with shame,
To think that I allowed
A heartless crowd to crucify,
A man by scorn unbowed.

(Enter BARABBAS. *Stands near the Cross.)*

BARABBAS

When Pilate asked the angry crowd
What he should do with me
They cried with voices that were loud
That I should be set free.

Barabbas is my well-known name,
And I deserved to die;
Yet Jesus took my place of shame
'Mid shouts of "Crucify."

(Enter SIMON OF CYRENE. *Stands near the Cross.)*

SIMON OF CYRENE

I am Simon of Cyrene,
Some men compelled me there
Up the road to Calvary
A wooden cross to bear.

I did not know the man who bowed
Beneath its heavy weight
Was sent to bear the guilt of all,
Their sins to expiate.

(Enter ROMAN SOLDIERS. *Stand near the tomb. Speak in unison or divide the parts by stanzas.)*

ROMAN SOLDIERS

We are Roman soldiers who
Stood by the Cross that day.
We saw darkness cover all
And heard this Jesus pray.

We are Roman soldiers who
Beheld the ground to shake;
Truly He's the Son of God
Who made the earth to quake.

We are Roman soldiers who
Beside the tomb kept guard
When the grave was tightly sealed
And with a stone was barred.

We are Roman soldiers who
  Became as men who died
When the Savior left the tomb
  Through a door that opened wide.

(Enter REPENTANT THIEF. *Stands looking at the Cross.)*

REPENTANT THIEF

I'm the thief whose cross was placed
  Beside the Savior's tree.
While another railed at Him
  I said, "Remember me."

I was guilty of my sin,
  My punishment a must;
But the Lord was innocent,
  His suffering was unjust.

Jesus said, "Today you'll be
  With Me in paradise."
I'm so glad He took me in
  By His great sacrifice.

(Enter MARY, *mother of Jesus. Stands near the Cross.)*

MARY

I'm the mother of my Lord,
  What privilege was mine
To be chosen in this way
  And bear the One divine.

As the mother of my Lord,
  My heart was broken sore;
On the day of Calvary
  I heard the crowd's uproar.

Then I saw Him lifted up.
  I heard His awful cry,
Watched Him suffer as no man.
  I watched Him bleed and die.

(Enter JOSEPH OF ARIMATHEA. *Stands near the tomb.)*

JOSEPH OF ARIMATHEA

I'm Joseph, friend of Jesus,
  I saw Him when He died;
I waited for the Kingdom;
  I saw Him crucified.

I went to beg of Pilate
   The body of my Friend.
I wrapped Him in pure linen,
   His burial to tend.

I placed Him in a garden,
   Within my new-made tomb;
I took His precious body,
   And laid it in the gloom.

(Enter Two Disciples. *Stand near the tomb. They may speak in unison, or parts can be divided by stanzas.)*

TWO DISCIPLES

We were walking on a road,
   Emmaus was its name;
While we reasoned of it all
   The risen Savior came.

We were saddened in our hearts;
   We talked of Him who died.
He had gone, we felt alone
   Since He was crucified.

When He came and walked with us
   We did not know Him there;
But He told us things of Him,
   The Scriptures all declare.

When He sat and ate with us
   He took and broke the bread.
Eyes were opened and we knew,
   He's risen from the dead!

(Enter Mary Magdalene. *Stands near the tomb.)*

MARY MAGDALENE

My name is Mary Magdalene;
   Christ did so much for me.
I followed and I watched from far
   That day at Calvary.

And very early in the morn
   I brought some spices rare;
To care for Him within the tomb,
   When they had placed Him there.

I saw the stone was rolled away;
My precious Lord was gone;
For He was risen as He said,
That resurrection dawn.

(Enter THOMAS. *Stands near the tomb.)*

THOMAS

I am called the doubting one,
For I did not believe,
When they told me, "He's alive,"
Their word I'd not receive.

I then said that I must see
Those precious hands, nail-scarred;
And I said that I must touch
That wounded side so marred.

But when I saw His precious face,
I felt my doubt relieved.
It was my Lord, alive I knew;
With all my heart believed.

READER: Now that you have met some of the people who knew Jesus, we would like you to meet Jesus if you don't already know Him as your Savior. He lives today and is still able to touch your life. He will make you a new creature, and your life will never be the same again. May He touch you.

His Promise

The grim cold winter has been with us,
Cold and barren as the day they laid Him in the tomb,
But the labor pain of spring is being felt
Bringing hope as wondrous as when He lay in the womb.
Soon bright colors and sweet scents,
Reminiscent of the oils He was anointed with,
Will be all around us filling us with untold joy.
Such was the day He rose from the dead.
Yes soon we'll walk in lush green grass
Swelling with flowers,
Beauty abounding as the garden of Eden
And we'll know His promise He'll keep
To take us home to everlasting peace.
We'll not lose hope and weep when winter comes
As the women by the grave,
For we know as the winter cocoon is spun
Spring waits to burst its bondage
And like our Lord, come again.

—Sandy Jordon

Tomorrow

The death of Jesus upon the Cross
Filled those who loved Him with such a loss;
Why must His life end this way?
Why was He destined to die this day?
He died to give us a new tomorrow,
Filled with hope and no more sorrow.
He died for all man's yesterdays,
To show the world another way.

—Carolyn Ray

19

Mary's Message

A Dramatic Monologue

(with live portraits)

by Bartie Jones

(Narrator is dressed like Mary, mother of Jesus, and stands to one side, spot-lighted. The other characters should be dressed appropriately. Follow lighting directions given for each portrait.)

Narration:

I knew
and then Elizabeth knew
and we waited together
for the Word to be made flesh.
Joseph was very good to me.
It was hard for him to accept, but
when he asked questions an angel
spoke to him in a dream. It seems
there was nothing more to be done
than to serve God by serving His Son.
And so it was.
Our family lived in Nazareth.
We had an open hearth
where people came to rest.
We offered our best love and care.
Joseph and Jesus helped them repair
or build something new.
Our children grew,
unfolding like flowers,
each day fairer with never a flaw.
We watched in awe.
Jesus was never ill,
and He roamed the hills
singing happily.
He made friends easily.
Eager and inquisitive,
He explored earth's delights,
studied, and played.
We prayed day and night.
For me, too, it was a learning
and growing time.
I knew in my heart
that Jesus was not really mine.

Live Portraits and Action:

(Spot on Elizabeth posed with hands reaching toward Mary.)

(Spot off.)

(Joseph steps into Mary's spot—puts arm around her.)

(Joseph leaves spotlight.)

(Joseph and boy Jesus with tools and another person with a broken chair.)

(Spot off.)

When He was 12
we took Him to Jerusalem. *(Spot on boy Jesus talking with a few*
We're not sure how He slipped away, *Jewish teachers.)*
but when we found Him, to our
surprise He was talking with teachers,
being wiser than the wisest of these. *(Spot off.)*
"Is He growing up already?"
I asked myself—and the answer came:
No, He is grown.
He was already stepping out on His
own.
There was a mystery there
I couldn't explain,
like a haunting halo
of distant pain.
He grew tall and wise
and His eyes pierced the heart.
He knew intuitively which part
needed loving and caring.
A ready compassion, rare for the
times,
flowed from Him like living water.
He was strong of limb. *(Spotlight on grown Jesus dressed in*
I wove a seamless robe for Him *a beautiful robe, His hands and arms*
before He left home to answer *raised. He is smiling.)*
His calling.
He walked many miles over the desert
and mountains, listening to God.
I heard He battled with the devil
all alone for 40 full days,
winning over great temptation.
God's ways are strange, indeed. *(Spot off.)*
The virtue He possessed and fully
used increased to an inner strength
and power
that came to flower
after His baptism—when beyond all
doubt—He knew just what He was
to do.
He chose 12 friends
to be with Him, several fishermen, *(Spot on Jesus with three or four of*
one lawyer, one tax collector, *the disciples.)*
and others.
They loved Him on sight,
followed Him eagerly, day and night.
He talked to many along the sea.
Sometimes He brought His friends to
me.

21

He considered all of them
God's assorted children.   *(Spot off.)*
Children—
oh, how I loved children.
It would have been so nice
to have had a grandchild,
but I knew Jesus would not marry
and rear children of His own.
So I found neglected ones to love   *(Spotlight on Jesus with five children*
and brought them home.   *seated around Him, one standing*
I cared for them, and He loved me   *with an arm around His shoulder, an-*
for it. (He loved them, too.)   *other on His lap . . . much like the fa-*
He helped me by telling them stories   *mous painting.)*
and praying for them, His energy
flowing, releasing a force that
renewed each child.   *(Spotlight off.)*
He told wonderful stories, not only
to children—He told all of us
stories—and we wondered at them
and learned so much from them.
He strengthened the weak
and healed the distraught,
so very many He healed and taught.
Many of us knew He was the Messiah
Though much of that was still
mystery.

Then, as time passed,
His new ways of thinking disturbed
some of the leaders, and they became
afraid.
They laid traps for Him and tried to
trick Him.
But He was wiser than they,
His words leaving them in
amazement.
Like a surgeon after a disease
He headed straight for Jerusalem,
leaving behind Him a trail of
miracles
that, one by one, traced what He had
done.
He spoke the true word of God,
stirring people's hearts
until a part of Him was in each one.
They beseeched *me* to convince *Him*
to take a place among the elders

22

and do some magician's deed
that would fill their need for the
spectacular.
His refusal raised their wrath
and they pursued Him with angry
shouts,
but He quietly took a path unknown
to them.
They knew not what He was about.
His power struck fear in them
and they began to plot,   *(Spotlight on Judas and two others*
even bribing Judas to betrayal.   *offering a bag of coins.)*
Judas may have been weak,
but He had great faith in Jesus
I do not condemn him—it was to be.   *(Spotlight off.)*
They took Him then, taunted and
tortured Him, put Him to shame,
tarnished His name.
I waited
and prayed.
I could not go with Him
to argue His case.   *(Spotlight on Jesus with soldiers on*
I could not defend Him   *each side, standing before Pilate.)*
nor go in His place.
I prayed,
"God, be merciful to Thy Son
He has only blessed and loved
everyone
oh, spare Him the agonies of the
Cross, I pray
yet—Thy will be done," I hastened to
say.   *(Spot off.)*
We followed Him up to the crest of
travail,
some shouting and spitting
and they drove in the nails!
I watched Him cry.
I watched Him die,
and my mind echoed Simeon's words
long past
that a sword would pierce through
my soul.
Here, at last, the prophecy was coming true.
Yet He prayed, "Father, forgive them,
for they know not what they do."
Such holy grace
in misery's face.

All bitterness left me then
and while others mourned
I remembered the night He was born   *(Spotlight on a young Mary, Joseph,*
when the shepherds came   *and Baby Jesus.)*
and a star had shone
to lead the way for the magi and say,
"This is a King,
give thanks and sing!"   *(Spotlight off.)*

What do you do? What do you say
when they crucify the son you love?
How do you pray?
   Believe in God
   and let Him go.
   Thy will be done,
   be still and know.
So I prayed as I stood by Calvary
until they lowered Him tenderly
and though they entombed Him
I did not stay.
I hastened to go back home
that day.
I knew in the very heart of me
that I would find Him in Galilee.
Waiting in a seamless robe He'd be   *(Spot on Jesus in robe standing in*
with the radiance of immortality.   *front of empty cross. The lighting can*
   And so it was!   *be very effective here by throwing all*
                                              lights on Jesus for 10 seconds and
                                              then blacking out totally for 20 sec-
                                              onds. This leaves the image in the
                                              audience's mind.)

Abide with Us—the Day Is Far Spent

An Easter Pageant with Ten Short Scenes

by Joyce McFarland

Time: Just a short time before the birth of Christ—until His ascension
Place: Emmaus and Jerusalem
Characters:

BENONI: *a middle-aged man from Emmaus*

DEBORAH: *the wife of Benoni*

CLEOPAS: *their young son, later seen as a youth, and then a grown man*

NATHAN: *neighbor of Benoni*

RABBI BEN EZRA: *the rabbi and teacher in the rabbinical school in Jerusalem*

SIMEON
BENJAMIN } *friends of Cleopas and students of Rabbi Ben Ezra*

PHARISEE 1

PHARISEE 2

JASON: *the crippled man Jesus healed*

JOSEPH OF ARIMATHEA
NICODEMUS } *secret believers of Jesus*

JONATHAN: *son of Cleopas*

REBECCA: *younger daughter of Cleopas*

VOICE

READER

Music:

Soft music—where this is indicated, organist or pianist plays to fit the mood of the scene.

Hymns—where these are indicated, such can be chosen to go with the scene, and can be sung by solo voices, duets, trios, or the choir.

Costumes:

Colorful biblical styles (These can be seen in pictures in Bible story books.)

Scenery and Properties:

Low stools, flowerpots, ferns, palms, plain tables, chests, and old-looking urns.

Backgrounds can be made with an artist's help if desired.

Slides can be effectively used for background, especially for the Crucifixion, Resurrection, Emmaus story, and the Ascension. (These can be obtained through local bookstores.)

Spotlights, using different colors, are also helpful.

(Soft background music.)

READER: Over 50 years had passed since the powerful arm of Rome had reached across the Mediterranean Sea and conquered Syria. A year later the grasping hand of that same arm reached down into Palestine, laying hold of Judea. Finally, its fingers seized Jerusalem, the Holy City of the Jews. What an hour of triumph that was for the great Roman Empire! But what an hour of bitter sorrow it was for the Jewish people! Taxes and tribute money were levied upon their income and their property. Even more ironic, they were required to pay for the privilege of being numbered among those who lived in a conquered land! Rome and her tyrannical rulers were determined to reduce all her subjects to the same level. Unquestioning obedience was demanded to her command. Thus it was believed that the pride of race and religion would be broken down. And so dark shadows fell across the whole of Palestine. They fell upon Jerusalem, upon its walls, its temple, its people. They spread out and lengthened until they enveloped the villages hidden in Judean hills and the little hamlets of northern Galilee. *(Lights in room go off gradually.)*

Outside Jerusalem, a main highway led to Joppa and from thence it went along the coast to Caesarea, headquarters for the city was an obscure village called Emmaus. Here lived Benoni, his wife, Deborah, and their small son, Cleopas.

(DEBORAH *enters, followed by* BENONI.)

BENONI: Deborah, life with this Roman rule is becoming unbearable!

DEBORAH: I know, dear. But has some new thing happened to cause you to be so troubled?

BENONI: It has! On the way to Jerusalem today, I was stopped by one of those Roman dogs. He ordered me to carry his baggage for him.

DEBORAH: But why did he ask you?

BENONI: One of his carriers was overcome with the heat.

DEBORAH: And did you obey?

BENONI: What else could I do? I carried the load! My kegs of olive oil had to be left behind until I could return for them. Fortunately they were still there when I got back.

DEBORAH: How tired you must be . . . if only . . .

(CLEOPAS *enters.*)

BENONI: Yes, dear, if only there were some hope. I pray that the promised Messiah will come soon!

(Sad music.)

CLEOPAS: Father, read to us tonight about the Messiah.

BENONI: I will, my son. Let me read the words of the prophet Jeremiah. He lived in a day that was something like our own ... "The days are coming, declared the Lord, when I will raise up to David a righteous Branch, a King who will reign wisely and do what is just and right in the land. In his days Judah will be saved and Israel will live in safety. This is the name by which he will be called: The Lord Our Righteousness."

(Family turns toward the east and prays.)

BENONI: "May God be gracious to us and bless us and make His face to shine upon us. O God, the nations have invaded Your inheritance—You have made us a reproach to our neighbors, the scorn and derision of those around us. Help us, O God our Savior, for the glory of Your name; deliver us and atone for our sins for Your name's sake."

FAMILY *(together)*: "Then we, Your people, the sheep of Your pasture, will praise You forever; from generation to generation we will recount Your praise."

Scene 2

(Hymn)

CLEOPAS: Here comes Nathan. He looks very excited!

BENONI: Good evening, friend. You had better sit down. You look all out of breath.

NATHAN: I cannot stay long. But I do want to tell you the news I heard in Jerusalem.

BENONI: The Holy City is always in turmoil these days!

NATHAN: Apparently three strangers entered the city yesterday. They were astrologers, magi, they call them. They inquired in several places with these words, "Where is he that is born King of the Jews? For we have seen his star and are come to worship him."

DEBORAH: What could they mean? Herod is king now!

NATHAN: I don't know what the words mean, but when Herod heard them, they say he grew purple with rage. He called in the priests and scribes demanding to know where Christ is to be born.

BENONI: Yes, and what then?

NATHAN: He commanded that the wise men be found and brought to the palace. Then he questioned them closely about the star. He also told them to return when they had found the child.

DEBORAH: King of the Jews ... Christ ... Messiah! Do you think that our prayers have already been answered?

READER: No more was heard of the searching magi. Nor was any more heard about a child, born to become King of the Jews. The months and the years passed by. The son of Benoni was a happy boy. Particularly did he love the Holy Scriptures taught to him by his father. When he was 12, it was decided to let him attend the rabbinical school held in the courts of the Temple in Jerusalem.

Scene 3

(RABBI BEN EZRA *enters from the left—boys from the right.*)

RABBI BEN EZRA: Let us read today from the prophet Isaiah concerning the promised Messiah.

ALL *(together):* "A shoot will come up from the stump of Jesse; from his roots a Branch will bear fruit. The Spirit of the Lord will rest on him—the Spirit of wisdom and of understanding, the Spirit of counsel and of power, the Spirit of knowledge and of fear of the Lord—but with righteousness he will judge the needy, with justice he will give decisions for the poor of the earth. He will strike the earth with the rod of his mouth; with the breath of his lips he will slay the wicked."

RABBI BEN EZRA: God's Word is true. He will send a deliverer to His people, Israel!

(RABBI *leaves—boys stand.*)

SIMEON: Our teacher does not seem like himself today.

BENJAMIN: Could it be that he has not gotten over the visit of that young boy from Nazareth?

CLEOPAS: Boy from Nazareth? I had not heard.

SIMEON: Some people from that town came to the city for the Feast of the Passover. Among them was a boy named Jesus. We happened to go by the court of Solomon and saw Him surrounded by the doctors.

BENJAMIN: Jesus was asking the teachers questions!

SIMEON: Every one of them were surprised at His wisdom and understanding!

CLEOPAS *(meditative attitude):* "The Spirit of the Lord will rest on him—the Spirit of wisdom and of understanding." God's Word is true. He will send a deliverer to His people, Israel.

READER: Twenty more years went by. The people of Palestine gradually grew accustomed to the Roman rule. Some still chaffed under the laws, but most of the population accepted them, feeling there was nothing else to do.

Then one day news began to filter into Jerusalem. A wild-looking man was preaching in the country near the Jordan River. It was reported that many went to hear him and that many were being baptized by him. Alarmed, the Jewish religious leaders sent priests and Levites to question him.

Cleopas, now grown to manhood, was a teacher of the Law. With his wife, he visited his father's home in Emmaus.

Scene 4

(BENONI *approaches from the left.* CLEOPAS *and* RACHEL *from the right.*)

BENONI: Cleopas, my son! It is good to see you! And my daughter, Rachel, too.

CLEOPAS: It is good to see you, too, Mother and Father.

RACHEL: Cleopas has been so excited over the recent news that he just had to come and tell you.

BENONI: News? Tell us all that you have heard, Son.

CLEOPAS: Have you heard about the man called John who is preaching in the wilderness near Jordan?

BENONI: Yes, several have gone from here to see and to hear him.

CLEOPAS: He was questioned the other day as to who he was. He said plainly, "I am the voice of one calling in the desert, 'Make straight the way for the Lord.'"

BENONI (*in awe*): "Comfort, comfort my people, says your God. A voice of one calling in the desert: 'Prepare the way for the Lord'; make straight in the wilderness a highway for our God."

CLEOPAS: You feel as I do, Father. But there is more. The next day, while John was baptizing, a man approached. John spoke to the people and he said, "Look, the Lamb of God who takes away the sins of the world."

BENONI (*face lifted*): "We all, like sheep, have gone astray, each of us has turned to his own way; and the Lord has laid on him the inquity of us all."

(*All turn toward Jerusalem, faces lifted.*)
(*Hymn*)

READER: Two years passed by. Reports were that John, the wilderness preacher, had been beheaded by Herod. More reports came in about Jesus of Nazareth who had been baptized by John. People followed Him like they did the baptizer. Twelve men had left their occupations to follow Him. The Pharisees were becoming agitated over the news they heard. The teachings of

29

this Jesus were in direct opposition to the laws and traditions of the fathers. More than that, the common people were following Him, as well as some of the rank. It was said that He could heal the sick, feed a multitude with a great lunch, still a storm on a raging sea. No doubt it was nothing but the exaggerated imagination of ignorant people, but it constituted a threat to the standing of the scribes and Pharisees. Cleopas did not see Him, but he had firsthand information. It happened like this.

Scene 5

(JASON, *a healed man, walks out right door—met by* PHARISEE 1 *and* PHARISEE 2 *in front.* CLEOPAS *approaching, hears.*)

PHARISEE 1: Stop there! What do you think you are doing?

PHARISEE 2: It is the Sabbath Day! It is against the law for you to carry your bed today!

JASON: He who made me well, said to me, "Get up, take your mat and walk."

PHARISEE 1: And why, pray tell, did He say that to you?

JASON: I was lying by the pool of Bethesda, waiting for the waters to be troubled. You know the custom—the first to step in after the waters are troubled will be healed.

PHARISEE 2: Yes, yes, go on.

JASON: A man came along. He spoke kindly to me and said, "Do you want to get well?"

PHARISEE 1: What happened then?

JASON: I said to Him, Sir, I have no one to put me into the pool after the waters are stirred. But just as I get to the pool's edge, another gets in before me.

PHARISEE 2: If that is the case, why are you walking now, carrying your mat? And on the Sabbath, too!

JASON: The man said to me to get up and take my mat and walk. And I, who have never walked for 38 years, walked!

CLEOPAS (*stepping forward*): And what was the man's name?

JASON: He is called Jesus, I believe.

(PHARISEES 1 *and* 2 *exit, muttering.*)

CLEOPAS (*to self, looking up*): "Then will the eyes of the blind be opened and the ears of the deaf unstopped. Then will the lame leap like a deer, and the tongue of the dumb shout for joy."

READER: The Jewish Feast of Tabernacles was a feast that every male was required by Jewish law to attend. So again Jesus came into Jerusalem. One day while there, Jesus went into the Temple and taught as one with great authority. A division soon arose among His listeners. Some believed He was a good man; others felt He was a prophet or even the Christ.

Cleopas desired greatly to see and hear Him, but again he was hindered. Two of his friends, Joseph of Arimathea and Nicodemus, told him what they had heard.

Scene 6

(JOSEPH *and* NICODEMUS *come down left aisle.*)
(CLEOPAS *walks out right door.*)

JOSEPH: You missed a lot by not being in the Temple today, Cleopas!

CLEOPAS: Did you see Him? Did you hear Him?

NICODEMUS: Yes, and He has been teaching openly in the Temple.

JOSEPH: The Sanhedrin is in a turmoil. He claims to teach a doctrine of the One who sent Him. He even said, "Yes, you know Me, and you know where I am from. I am not here on My own, but He who sent Me is true. You do not know Him, but I know Him because I am from Him and He sent Me."

NICODEMUS: Many believed on Him then. Jesus said to them, "If you hold to My teaching, you are really My disciples. Then you will know the truth, and the truth will set you free."

CLEOPAS: The prophet Isaiah said, "The Spirit of the Sovereign Lord is on me, because the Lord has anointed me to preach good news to the poor. He has sent me to bind up the brokenhearted, to proclaim freedom for the captives, and release for the prisoners."

JOSEPH: Yes, the prophecy surely describes this man. Many believe He is the Christ. But our religious leaders are disturbed. They feel He is an imposter and a blasphemer.

CLEOPAS: I have never seen Him. I have never heard Him. But I believe He is the Christ. He is our Messiah. (*Looks up with awe.*)

(*Hymn*)

READER: And thus it was that Cleopas became a disciple of the one called Jesus. Later events only served to strengthen his faith.

From Bethany came the story of how Lazarus, a friend of Jesus, had died. His sisters were mourning his death. Then Jesus came, and upon being taken to the burial place, had called to the young man to come forth. The report was verified by many that the boy had been dead four days but that he had immediately come forth, graveclothes and all.

The time drew near to the annual Feast of the Passover. It was rumored that Jesus was in a caravan coming from Galilee to Jerusalem for the event. Feelings ran high that the kingdom of God would soon be set up and the power of Rome defeated. Cleopas, coming for the noon meal, found excited children waiting for him.

Scene 7

JONATHAN: Father, you should have been with us! We saw Him! We saw Jesus!

CLEOPAS: You did, my son?

JONATHAN: Abner's father and others heard that He was coming. Many people started toward the city gates. We ran along with them!

REBECCA: And, Father, the people took palm branches and began to sing out, "Hosanna, blessed is he who comes in the name of the Lord. Blessed is the King of Israel!"

JONATHAN: We shouted hosanna, too! Do you think He really will be the king?

RACHEL: Do you think the time has come for the Christ to set up His kingdom?

CLEOPAS: Perhaps it will be so, and I should be glad if it would happen. But somehow, I do not feel the time is now. There are many who are even trying to get such an event to pass now.

READER: The next few days were busy ones. Along with the excitement of the Passover Week was an undercurrent of tension. Jesus was teaching in the Temple. Again Cleopas did not chance to see Him, but he heard what He said. Jesus was said to have spoken these strange words: "Walk while you have the light. Put your trust in the light while you have it so that you may become the children of light. I have come into the world as a light, so that no one who believes in Me should stay in darkness." Many of the chief rulers even believed on Jesus but did not confess Him openly. Cleopas continued to believe in his heart that Jesus was the Messiah.

Scene 8

(NICODEMUS, JOSEPH, *and* CLEOPAS *meet in front.*)

NICODEMUS: I shall never forget how I visited Him one night. My mind was full of questions. While we talked, He told me what I should do to inherit eternal life! But I do not dare to mention these things before the Pharisees.

JOSEPH: My position in the council would be in danger. Think what that would mean! It would involve my family and also my friends.

CLEOPAS: I have considered all this. But I for one must confess Him openly. Ever since that day when I first believed His words, I have been free! The fears of this life and of death are gone! And I will follow Him always.

(Soft music.)

READER: Then came the day of shock and disbelief. Jesus had been arrested. *(Somber music.)* He had been arraigned before Herod, then Pilate, and then

Herod again. At the insistence of the angry mob of scribes and Pharisees, He was condemned to be crucified. Many of His own disciples fled in fear. Then on the day before the Sabbath, Jesus was forced to climb the hill called Golgotha and there He was crucified. A few of His disciples and friends followed at a distance. This time Cleopas was there, too.

Scene 9

(Mob and friends gather.)

CLEOPAS: I cannot understand all of this! But I shall believe in Him still. He is the Christ! This is what the prophet Isaiah must have meant when he wrote the words: "He was despised and rejected by men, a man of sorrows, and familiar with suffering. Like one from whom men hid their faces he was despised and we esteemed him not. ... But he was pierced for our transgressions, he was crushed for our iniquities; the punishment that brought us peace was upon him, and by his wounds we are healed. ... Because he poured out his life unto death, and was numbered with the transgressors. For he bore the sin of many, and made interecession for the transgressors."

(Sad music.)

READER: Sad hours of darkness and despair followed. Fear lay like a cloud over the city. Then early in the morning of the first day of the week, women went to the tomb to anoint the body of Jesus with spices. When they arrived they found the stone rolled away from the tomb where Jesus had been laid. An angel appeared and questioned them thus: "Why do you look for the living among the dead? He is not here; He has risen! Remember how He told you, while He was still with you in Galilee: 'the Son of Man must be delivered into the hands of sinful men, be crucified and on the third day be raised again.'"

    The women remembered then and hurried away to tell the disciples and all the rest.

(Hymn)

Scene 10

READER: Thus it was that two men walked along the road to Emmaus the afternoon of that same day. But let us listen to one of them as he tells the story to his family afterward.

RACHEL: Cleopas, your face is radiant! Why are you so joyful when everyone else is mourning and sad?

REBECCA: Father, you look just like I felt that day we saw Jesus and sang hosannas to Him!

JONATHAN *(with brotherly importance):* He already told me, for I was waiting for him by the gate. You will never believe what he has to tell, little sister!

CLEOPAS: Yes, it seems almost unbelievable, but it is true. Your grandfather, Benoni, and I were going out of the city toward Emmaus. He is old and I did not want him to travel alone. As we walked along we could not help but feel sad.

You know that both of us believed Jesus to be the Christ. God had revealed it to us so many times! We tried to reconcile the events with prophecy. Just then a Stranger drew near and walked along with us. Before we knew it, He was comforting us with words from the Scriptures. *(Pause.)* I shall never forget how I felt *(pause);* everything seemed to straighten out as He spoke; my heart burned within me!

We drew near to your grandparents' home, children. The Stranger acted as if He was going farther. We urged Him to stay with us, for it was late in the day. More than that, somehow it seemed we really needed His presence just then. He agreed and came into the house. Your grandmother brought us some food, and strangely, He took His place at the head of the table—just like the master of the house ordinarily would. Then He took the bread, and looking up, He blessed it. Suddenly, though I had never seen Him closely before, I knew Him. He was Jesus, my risen Savior and my Lord!

(Hymn)

READER: Jesus remained here on earth for about 40 days, appearing to His disciples at different times and in different places. Then one day, He called them together and they followed Him up the mountain called Olivet. There He spoke to them for the last time. Listen to His words!

VOICE: "All authority in heaven and on earth has been given to me. Therefore go and make disciples of all nations, baptizing them in the name of the Father and of the Son and of the Holy Spirit, and teaching them to obey everything I have commanded you. And surely I will be with you always, to the very end of the age." "But you will receive power when the Holy Spirit comes on you; and you will be my witnesses in Jerusalem, and in all Judea and Samaria, and to the ends of the earth."

READER: It is recorded that the followers of Jesus came down from Mount Olivet and returned to Jerusalem. They went again to the Upper Room and stayed there in prayer. They remained in that place waiting, as Jesus had told them to. When the Day of Pentecost was fully come, just as had been promised, they "were filled with the Holy Spirit and began to speak in other languages as the Spirit enabled them."

Among these people, there probably were Joseph of Arimathea, Nicodemus, Cleopas and his family.

They found that the Guest of the Emmaus way had come to abide forever in the yielded hearts of those who loved Him.

34

We Remember You

A. S. C.

Annette Seaton Colbert

1. Here, at this ta - ble,___ we wor - ship in Your
2. We eat this bread, Lord,___ the sym - bol of Your
3. We drink this cup, Lord,___ the sym - bol of Your
4. Lord, we ex - alt You,___ our res - ur - rect - ed

pres - ence; Per - fect Re - deem-er,___ the cho - sen Lamb of
bod - y; Wound-ed and bro - ken,___ once hang-ing on a
shed blood, Pre - cious and ho - ly,___ Love's of - fer - ing for
Sav - ior; Seat - ed in pow - er___ at God's right hand on

God.___ We look by faith to the path of death You
tree;___ Bear - ing the judg - ment for all in - iq - ui -
sin;___ Mak - ing a - tone - ment to free men from with -
high;___ Now in - ter - ced - ing, for - give - ness to pro -

trod.___ With hum-ble rev - 'rence, we re - mem-ber You.
ty.___ With hum-ble rev - 'rence, we re - mem-ber You.
in.___ With hum-ble rev - 'rence, we re - mem-ber You.
vide.___ With hum-ble rev - 'rence, we re - mem-ber You.

Jesus Christ Is Alive

tain Him, It can - not con - quer me; And the pow - er of sin is
I live And I'll nev - er for - sake. Flood or flame shall not o- ver -

bro - ken And the spir - it is free to sing of Je - sus.
whelm you all the way.___ I will take you through to glo - ry,

Je - sus, Je - sus Christ is a - live; Je - sus is a -
glo - ry" Je - sus Christ is a - live; Je - sus is a -

live for - ev - er - more.___
live for - ev - er -

more.___

___ Je - sus is a - live for - ev - er - more.___

Jesus, Our Savior, Lives

Mildred S. Edwards

Arthur H. Messiter

1. Be glad! Be glad! And sing on Eas-ter Day.
2. He lives! He lives! Yes, Je-sus, our Sav-ior, lives.

Hallelujah! What a Savior!

Philip P. Bliss

Harlan Moore

1. "Man of sor - rows," What a name ____ For the Son of
2. Bear-ing shame and scoff - ing rude, ____ In my place con-
3. Guil-ty, vile, and help - less we; ____ Spot-less Lamb of
4. Lift-ed up was He to die; ____ "It is fin - ished,"
5. When He comes, our glo - rious King, ____ All His ran - somed

God who came ____ Ru - ined sin - ners to re-claim! ____
demned He stood; ____ Sealed my par-don with His blood. ____
God was He. ____ "Full a - tone-ment!" Can it be? ____
was His cry. ____ Now in heav'n ex - alt - ed high, ____
home to bring, ____ This our glo - rious song we'll sing: ____

Hal - le - lu! ____ Hal - le - lu! ____ Hal - le - lu! ____ What a Sav - ior!

God Is Not the God of the Dead

D. W.

Dan Whittemore